To Lili
with love

Ruth

Thanks For Caring

The Mother's Breast
and the Father's House

The Mother's Breast and the Father's House

Poems by Reed Whittemore

 HOUGHTON MIFFLIN COMPANY BOSTON
1974

First Printing   w

Library of Congress Cataloging in Publication Data

Whittemore, Reed, 1919–
   The mother's breast and the father's house.

   I. Title.
PS3545.H868M6   811'.5'4   74–12180
ISBN 0–395–19840–2
ISBN 0–395–19921–2 (pbk.)

Printed in the United States of America

Among the new poems, "Let It Blow" first appeared in *The New
Yorker*, and the following first appeared in *The New Republic*:
"The Mother's Breast and the Father's House," "All Over Town,"
"Money," "Ode to New York," Foxy Loxy's Christmas Happiness,"
"The Washington Gloom-Doom-Stomp," "Oh There You Are,"
"Science Fiction," "Eat-Mit-Fingah Shaggy," and "For the Life
of Him and Her." The old poems have been selected from three
volumes published by the University of Minnesota Press (*An
American Takes a Walk*, 1956; *Poems New and Selected*, 1967;
Fifty Poems Fifty, 1970), three volumes published by the
Macmillan Company (*The Self-Made Man*, 1959; *The Boy from
Iowa*, 1962; *The Fascination of the Abomination*, 1963), and
a volume published by Reynal and Hitchcock, Inc. (*Heroes and
Heroines*, 1946). Thanks to these publishers for granting
permission to use the poems here.

The same care which covers the seed of
the tree under tough husks and stony cases,
provides for the human plant the mother's breast
and the father's house.

— from "Domestic Life"
by Ralph Waldo Emerson

Contents

New Poems (1970–1974)

Old Poems (1945–1970)

New Poems
1970-1974

The Mother's Breast and the Father's House

Lectures lectures cometh two lectures

    Lecture One
Here we are on this planet
                    (folks)
Life is too long
It needs sleep to fill in
And sex and money and birthdays
And most of all faith

To achieve faith one must suffer for decades
And to suffer one must get up early and
    raise a family and go to work
Suffering is middle class
It was invented by Benjamin Franklin
It begins with the search for a loaf of bread and ends
    with funeral expenses
It is composed of ten parts body
    and five parts bank account
It is caused by God
Being part of His clumsy plan to extract positive charges
    from His creation in anticipation of something
    better

He gave the thing over to Franklin when Job failed Him
And now the wives are in charge

Wives suffer first since marriage is designed to route
    the pain slowly through the female to the male
    and then to the children and the dog
Wives suffer in childbirth in giving suck in cooking
    feeding cleaning screaming hating and washing
    dishes

And then they cry so that the husband buys another car and
　　a larger house and floats an eight percent loan and
　　thinks of salt flats
So that the older children who are watching and listening
　　and hating make up their minds that they are not
　　going to live like *that*
And run off with their peers to suffer in city pads
Thereby spreading suffering momentarily beyond the confines
　　of the middle class
But coming back soon broke and broken to suffer properly in
　　the home

And all of this breeds faith in the home
Faith is despair spelled backwards
Despair is what distinguishes men from rocks
Which can sit in the sun and rain for ages and not be
　　bothered
Rocks grow more lichen than men can
They don't flinch on the first of the month
They don't drink too much or get put in hospitals or commute
　　fifty miles to work monday through friday
Or weep at the horror of waking up

They lead a nice quiet nonlife with no charlie horses or
　　connubial bliss
Whereas men have to put up with approximately twenty thousand
　　days of continuous disaster
Which causes despair
And produces novels and doctors
And relentlessly breeds (as I say) faith
Mostly in the middle aged
　　　　　　　　　(poor saps)
How they hang on
They sit in the living room while the government robs
　　them blind
They eat beef stroganoff while the one hundred biggest
　　corporations devise a new way to cheapen their
　　toilet paper

They go to the movies while their children make wax
       images of them and stick pins in them
And they pay pay until the wallet dies and the
       checkbook dies and they stare at the ceiling
       sleepless wondering whom they have forgotten
       to pay
          leading to

Lecture two

If you take an ordinary fly that is buzzing around your
       head
And kill him by whacking your head severely with a book
You have the germ of an illuminating lecture on the care
       of the self
Another way is to take off your clothes at a party in
       order better to discuss
Human frailty

But do not
         (folks)
Miss the point
You may be sad
But you are not frail

You are tough

Your seemingly small mind is in truth an enormous warehouse
       devoted to documenting and buttressing the persistence
       of you

Stuff with the dust of decades is in it
Books faces tears fears
Loves hates games names
All in relation to
You

It is reported that a significant seventy-year-old alcoholic on Cape Cod

       can recall every purchase of liquor he has made since
       he was fourteen
Colors odors textures travel incredible distances with us
Even the weakest among us is a sort of god of preservings of
       that which would be wholly trivial if it were not ours
Attics we are capable of crowding with worn memories of shoes
       and hockey sticks
Pages and pages we shore up of ghostly banality
Acres of images of the dead the lost the irretrievably past
       but not
Forgotten we plant in that submarginal country we can neither
       live in nor leave
Where the soul
Goes to brood out of the dailiness

There it sits on rocks and looks at the waste sky
Keeping the faith

Which is why we lecturers are sometimes uneasy as we travel
       the circuit patting sweet selves on the head
The selves on closer inspection turn out to be
       gobble-ups
Yet at least there remains the inexhaustible fact of the self
It doesn't leave
Nor does it walk into the living room on a friday night and suffer
       a cheap metamorphosis into an upper or lower class fruitfly
It persists
Its essence is that it persists

So
       (folks)
You whose self first got its notions of self in the bosom of a six-week
       $4000 Xmas
Shouldn't imagine that you can now walk breezily incognito into a
       dried fish commune
You may learn to live briefly in poverty in a hillock of hair
But you will not be able to destroy the country club because you still
       have a locker

You may be able to avoid taking a job as stockbroker or advertising
     copy writer
But you will not be able to maintain your moral edge longer than your
     tennis figure

Life is long

And the longer it is the surer it is to take us back where we started
In the excessively neat house with the hedge and mortgage

We will not escape what we are praying to escape
Nor divest ourselves of the qualities in ourselves that we despise
And we might therefore have a go at a very long drunk or an even
     longer death
If it were not that we would not then be the optimists that we are
And presumably will remain even if the feds double the income tax

For ours is the kingdom of the 10% joy the 15% satisfaction the
     20% love
That exists and will continue to exist beyond all misery

With the wisdom of necessity we
Will breathe
       hang on
          let be

And there is no lecture three

Where the Path Ends

The path ends at the cabin.
Where it ends it ends; one goes no farther.
Out beyond has the color and texture of Cotton Mather,
A sternness, a death fix.

But there's a sun patch,
And a small atheist bird flits about.
Levity.

To be out, looking in,
Is to think of sin,
And how one should go to church or kneel or offer up something
        from an airport gift shoppe.

But to be in? Looking out?
How would it be to see cabin and path and two-legged types
With the dark interior vision of an old stump?

Many of the two-legged ones do indeed imagine that they see out from
        those depths.
They are severe at parties.
They stand talking with drink in hand of the id and the afterlife,
Of bottomless canyons of soul.

They have not been out past the path's end either.

They know no more of the dark than any child.
They project their own melodramatic notions out past the path's end,
A common fallacy.

Could it be that behind the demons of tree trunks,
And the glacial stonery,
Could it be that the soul of the wild chews placidly like a cow?

I project the image.

I fear death,
But once when it was close to me it was cowlike,
It went moo.

The cabin may be the darker place.

Marriage

Well there was the story of the little pig
Who grew up to be an enormously handsome but anal hog
And was always sweeping and dusting the slops
So that the widow Brown thought she was going mad
And would clomp out to the sty and scream at the hog
Is this a sty or not? Are you a hog or not?
So that the hog got to feeling bad
And one day when she was beating him good he rose on his hind legs
And stared at her hard and said honey look in my eyes
Don't you see I am your old farmer Brown
Who with all my sins upon me fell in the hay baler
And am doomed to walk the earth in the form of a hog
For a certain period?

            Well the widow looked
And yes she thought she could really see in those red red eyes
The familiar lascivious look of her old mate
So she said goddam it you old bastard you won't let me be *yet*
To which he replied equably want to bet?
                    and thereupon
Vanished all half ton of him
Making the widow Brown shake with chagrin
Thinking of what might have been had for him in Austin Minn

Well the clouds floated over the Brown farm
The seasons paced through the fields
And the widow sat inside drinking sadness from her bitter cup
Until she grew dead and rose to heaven where was her old hub
Looking himself but two percent saintly
Who said goddam it you old bitch now you're following *me*

And she said shut up you swine
And he said they didn't turn you into swine because you always
       were swine

And they glowered evenly there amid pearls
Until God sauntered and said swine you must sublime
All that

All what? said widow Brown
All what? said farmer Brown

Hurry down said God to the Sublimate Station

Which they did

And were each duly issued an aeon's supply of the other
Chopped grated sautéed stuffed salted and warmed over
So that they could and did one another gloriously
Grind gnaw chomp
From chop to shank from knuckle to hind quarter
Including the mind the spirit the ego the id the will
Not to mention the conscience the oedipus complex the mother fix and
     leftover marital swill
Did eat and eat and eat in a heavenly sty
And were satisfied wholly
And were undiminished wholly
And were shrunken by not one hunk in the hump of their faithful malice
Because this was after all heaven and God understood

That a marriage needed a little help if two critturs
Were to cleave unto one another
                    through sickness
                          and bitters

Haiku #1

A traditional haiku has seventeen syllables
Hasn't it?

Psalm

The Lord feeds some of His prisoners better than others.
It could be said of Him that He is not a just god but an indifferent
      god.
That He is not to be trusted to reward the righteous and punish the
      unscrupulous.
That He maketh the poor poorer but is otherwise undependable.

It could be said of Him that it is His school of the germane that
      produced the *Congressional Record*.
That it is His vision of justice that gave us cost accounting.

It could be said of Him that though we walk with Him all the days of
      our lives we will never fathom Him
Because He is empty.

These are the dark images of our Lord
That make it seem needful for us to pray not unto Him
But ourselves.
But when we do that we find that indeed we are truly lost
And we rush back into the safer fold, impressed by His care for us.

All Over Town

All over town they are shouting next door,
Pushing buttons, letting the noise out,
Letting it float over grass to neighbors.

It takes two kinds,
Shouters and neighbors.

And it takes days with the windows open,
Heat, an illusory calm,
So that the sound will carry and the ear be the more struck.

And it takes unquantified energy out of deep holes
That has come to belong to no one, but to neighbors,
Who must listen and hear its loss and themselves feel the loss.

And carry on with their goldfish.

Nobody cares of course. It is only that
Everybody cares terribly. It is only that
Those must shout and these must listen

And the grass in between, and the emptiness.

Let It Blow

Let it blow, said the union of amalgamated winds,
And let it drip, said the cloud trust.
Where is there an end to it,
The self-interest?
— Whither my feet takest me I find lobbying,
Invented by Joseph Lobby,
Who wrote a nonpartisan editorial in behalf of his own candidacy
     for alderman in a tiny New England slum housing development
     in 1802.

Now each purple mountain majesty requires a private sunrise.
We pass individually unto grace, cutting each other on the thruway,
Singing the brotherhood of one.

Let it blow;
Let the assorted selves drop leaflets against litter,
Picket the morning.

Who will volunteer to park in a bus stop?
Foul the word supply?

— The right of the people to keep and bear arms shall not be infringed
Nor other rights of the righteous
So that the pharmaceutical firms may suck forever ˙
On the inner heart of our headache.

How can a nation of smart cookies be so dumb?
Did Jefferson do it? Hamilton? Thoreau maybe?

— I look into the kindly eyes of my anarchist soul mate,
She (he) dreaming of a Greek isle with her (his) American
     Express card,
She (he) wanting 400 hp and a water bed
     (and a mountain, a guru, and an independent income).

15

Not an institution in this country is not betrayed by its souls
    in residence.

Who is left to pull the weeds from the Xerox machine?
Where will we find the manpower to carry this week's privateering to
    the town dump?

— Let it blow,
And let the associations for the preservation of freedoms publish the
    unexpurgated results
At a profit.

Writer and Reader

You:
I don't know what I will say to you
As I speak to you
But I need to invoke you
That I may say to you
What it is I will say

I know that behind your eyes
That I cannot see
And your voice
That I cannot hear
Are your thoughts
That I cannot penetrate

I postulate that you hear me and are touched
You reach out to me our eyes meet
So that I speak to you and I say what it is that I say
To you only

Therefore:
What I say to you is you only
You of my need
Who are all that is substantive
In what I say

* * *

And I predicate:
You are like me
Let us touch
Let us take off clothes

* * *

But my dear:
Though I hold you in sweet bondage
And would gladly devote the rest of my life to adoring you
I find you contemptible
Because of your flaws
The ones I expose
With incisive prose

You are weak and submissive
Conventionally conformable
Institutionally malleable
Cravenly pragmatic
Middle class
Genteel

I will make you strong
I will make you compassionate

I will make you what I am not as a way to my need
Which is to change myself into that into which I will change you
In order that when I speak to you you will hearken
And when I cleave unto you you will cleave unto me
And we gloriously strong and compassionate two
Will be one

And not middle class

     *   *   *

Therefore sit:
You are my words my music we must collaborate
In this venture agreeing that truth

Is not a rock
But a tone a manner a ringing concurrently ringing
In your soul and mine as we sit in our garden communing
Ringing true
Let us agree then
That the truth is in A flat

It is also in bare feet
Let us agree
That it is eastern and nonrepresentational
And extracurricular and in free verse
Let us agree
It is not in the army
Nor the family

Time is its enemy

And the forty-hour week

Let us agree
To intensity
Devoid of irony
Out of history
Free

So that truly the truth may be
What sayeth we

      *   *   *

Yes
Whatever it is of which we are wholly convinced
Must be true
Such as our integrity

We are unique in this there are no
Others nobody anywhere ever remotely as
Honest as we

We feel more
And deeper
We are alone in the depth of our depth
Of sensibility
See?

      *   *   *

But as I speak to you in this vein your image recedes from me
I had to bring your supplies up here on foot
It is thoughtless of you to walk out on a Saturday night

     *   *   *

And now a bird in the wood is singing of itself
Over and over unchangingly the same notes
From the same branch

As if in the life of bird and song and branch
There were no other grace than to persist

And God would cry down at a false note
And the branch would crack
And the bird and the world would end in a wild rage

At a false note
That the bird in its pride might utter against its own throat

But knows better

Observing the rule of the self
That it now would teach me
Out of the inner cell
Of its mystery

The Learning Soul

Each soul should go to its own college
And look at a kindred soul there freely,
As if the tutors had all been dismissed and the law books sold,
And no high magistrate could intrude with rulings.

It should strip the dear kin down sweetly and leisurely,
Meditate on each part and reassemble,
Then stand back judiciously as at a gallery
To judge proportion and balance, and guess at meaning.

Last, it should do what it must do if it is truly
A free soul; it should enter into its slavery fully,
Giving without reserve its dearest reserve
To the kindred one. So the lonely tutors keep saying.

Rocks

Is the world a dream?
— The waking is always to facts that are like rocks
And lives that are like rocks
To poverty that is not an abstraction but a great rock
To sickness and loneliness loss and emptiness
That are all rocks

Is love a dream?
— It would be clever to say that one must climb up the other
          rocks to arrive at the love rock
Or that love is a rock hidden in life's moss

But to say such things is to be out of love

If there is love
                    and I think there is
It survives the saying only with difficulty
It needs prayer rather
I will not play with it

But of the rocks that are hateful to man and surround him
So that it is as if he were deep in a great rock canyon and calling
          for help and only to rocks
Of such rocks it is safe to speak
They need to be hammered at through the ages by man in his
          prison suit
They need to be broken up into smaller and smaller rocks

Afternoon Music

In the heat of the day a crow is waking up sinners.
They sleep too much.
He bestirs them and flies surly off and they lapse into sin again.
The sun is straight overhead, comatose.
If God is awake he has gone for the day to the city.
But the rocks are talking, the damned noisy rocks. The big one
Is telling the little one of the old days
In the north when the ice of Saskatchewan
Gave them a *big* ride.
One of the little ones won't credit it, knowing that nothing
Of consequence budges, the essence is lump.
He sniffs and the big rock sniffs and the crow comes back
For more preach. The wind rises, the ferns shake,
Somebody miles in the sky starts a mower,
And all through the long afternoon the closet of memories
Empties:

How the child won his letter at camp for naming ten flowers,
But flunked trees,
And the counsellor urged him to chew his milk,
And the daddy with very red ears told him life's facts
But left out the good part,
And the mommy was drunk and unhappy,
And the sun beat down.

Did he name ten ferns?

And how the man lay in an orchard next to an airstrip,
And it was dry, and the messkits clanked.
And how the man died a death one year but they wouldn't bury him,
And how he woke once more but was changed,
And how the flesh lay old in the sun
And the sweat ran down.

Fragments, colors. The texture of path,
The scratch of grass,
Sand in bathing suits, cobwebs in hair,
Mildew, bicycles.

Like notions at Woolworth's,
Aisle after aisle, in the heat, the quiet,
The season's accumulation
Piling up, spilling over.

But the rock,
The big rock,
Says Saskatchewan ice
Is different
From your everyday ice.
And now an enormous fat cloud climbs on the pines.
Faint thunder, a cool, a stillness — and *crack*.
The storm comes.
A closing of windows.

             *   *   *

All those enormous phalluses in the forest
Frighten an old mind.
So much thrust.
Such rude.
And the weight of detritus, the bulk of loss:
Unseemly.
            Who will clear it?

Somebody should have been put in charge, maybe a bishop.
Somebody ought to be *running* this place, a few rules,
Decorum.
            It simply won't do
To be wild all the time. Bad for the blood
And the glands and kidneys, bad for the brain.
Breeds idiots, makes suicides.

            The flesh loses tone.

The kulch goes to flab.

What are we coming to?

Rot, hollowness.

Not a sound tree in that stand.

No, you young bucks
With the flies always open
And eyes hanging out at the sight of a little titty,
Staying up all hours, drinking, smoking, racing those
Hopped-up jobs with the high rearends, swearing, shitting around,

You think you know everything,
                              and won't do a lick,
And think that somebody owes you because you've got looks
And muscle
And can play guitar.
                    You think wrong.
Time you learned.

But the trees shine in the rain and now they are innocents
Out of an idyll,
Each in its reticence drawing its sustenance, adding its substance,
     heedlessly serving,
In the way of primitive life, the designed life,
And the miracle of their growing is part of the glory of

God? Come off it.
Let fact gnaw a bit:
                    them trees is trees.

          *   *   *

But the mind thinks god, sees god
In every wet chipmunk.
The wet piles up.
The eaves drip.
And the mind sits at the window at prayer
Trying to reach the wet secret, asking

Is it that the mind inside at the window is watching the
Outside,
Or that the outside is watching the
Inside?

Deep philosopher. Bishop, Pope.

But the big rock says to the little rock,
My God it's wet,
Never saw anything like it,
                                    we'll be lucky
If it don't freeze in the twenty-fifth century,
                                              maybe sooner;
Should have brought a hat.

        *   *   *

Maybe a soul is driven to solitude out of the loneliness
Of the world, a touching and parting,
Is driven out of the silences of rooms
To the woods as if to a grand illicit romance
Hoping for someone to fall from the sky and talk and be
Close; so that it preens itself
By the window, and lifts its head a bit.

And the woods presence watches.
It sees the cribbed soul as a flirt with a nameless sadness,
And does what it can to comfort the soul, and the soul
Is comforted.

And maybe the soul must then open up and reveal itself,
Every sin and failing,
                          beads on a string,
Sighing,
Raging against the stench of success,
Grieving that love went to lunch and returned not,
Lapsing into long silences, fathomless glances.

So that:

After the rain has stopped and the sun has come out,
The soul at its window is deep in its solipsism,
Watching for watchers,
Feeling a presence it knows not,
Yet knows with such intimacy that it knows of the knowing,
Knows the knowing of rain,
Of trees,
Of rock, fern, flower, and how without watching
They watch,
And how without knowing
They know;
And how if one sits by the window watching the rain
It is like an old film,
A very old film of the mind
With the mind on the screen
And the mind in the audience watching the screen,
Each watching each,
And the Wurlitzer playing.

       *   *   *

But the little rock said to the big rock, Pappy,
Don't you think something's missing out here since that nice ice left?
Yup, said Pappy.
What is it?
Well, said Pappy,
Mainly it's rocks.
Left 'em all in Saskatchewan.
Can't run a rock farm
Without rocks.

Love My Dog

Let me truth you.
In New Hampshire in July it is cool, hot, clear, cloudy.
Birds sing and are silent.
The still road passes.

I will add that a birch tree grows by my loneliness.
I am male, college-educated, middle-aged.
I speak to you late in the century
And the language by which I might speak to you has departed me.

Listen:
Life is sickness and sadness
And health and joy.
In the morning the sun comes up.
Each man has a childhood,
Eats peanut butter,
Bestirs himself among girls, rides bikes, lies,
And teachers in hundreds of classrooms tell him to whisper not.
He is good in his earnestness, bad in his selfishness,
        all-American, boy-man,
And he cannot speak.

See the mole on his chin, the slight bowleggedness. See the wife.
Note the bills on his desk,
The pencils, nail clippers, coffee cups, paper clips.
The full wastebasket witness. This clutter
Is a man of the 20th century.

So the earth spins through the heavens,
The ferns are silent,
And the man walks out before breakfast
In the hush premonitory
Hearing the beat of the blood, the shoes' crunch.
And in quiet his soul

Speaks to the earth saying, On with it,
Light, life,
On with it, get on with it, on
Through the wood
To the frame house, the eggs, the juice,
The middle class life,
The silence.

* * *

Let me truth you.
It is hard for a statement to reach unto heaven.
Life is a breath over breakfast verily,
The *Times*.
Man pares his nails and lies down.
His senses belong to Sulzberger.
The truths that there be he may fold and dismiss
But they follow him, yes, they follow him all the days of his life
   and discomfort him,
The Chilean problem, the slump in textiles.
Life is long says a well-known medico
And all through the house
The house of the body
Not a creature is stirring
Except for the teeth
That grind slowly
So that at nine o'clock
God asks "What want you?"
And the man cannot speak
And God is impatient
And speaks from a fern leaf
Saying

"Who are you?
Why did you happen to think you could or should speak?
Let the *Times* speak
And the Department of Sociology of the University of Chicago
And other accredited modern institutions,
Let them speak as in any event they will speak

And let your soul if you have a soul
And your will if you have a will
Lie down in their glandular caves
And be still."

And God speaks no more.

And the man walks forth in the sun, that many adventures
May have him.

    *   *   *

Therefore:
On the road of his fate diurnal
He meeteth a crone yclept Virus
Who speaks to him sharply, pokes him, prods him, vanishes.
He grows ill,
Is healed by a two-legged Pill
But tackled by Invoice
Whom he pays till his Money
Parts from him, he is alone and the Unpaid shriek
In his face, one repossessing shoes, another wristwatch
And a third with the look of a priest stripping credit cards from him
So that he presses on weary, soul faint, doubting of Justice
When suddenly
Out of the ground
The saxes, the fiddles
Rise and their name is Legion
And they play as in axle grease
With vaseline voices over them singing, singing

     Bless the U.S. Mess, Miss

Singing

     Ain't A-Gonna Sell My Central City Short

Singing

     Take a poet home to supper if you're serving corn

Singing

Love Me, Love My Dog

And dozens of other favorites
Several at once
So that:

The man lies down.

The Monster Mortgage kicks him and he winces not.

The Insurance Slugs suck at him and he flinches not.

The Tax Leeches, the Doctor Ticks, the Utilities Lice and
    the Car Worms
They eat at him slowly and gravely and he talks not back.

> *Love my dog, sweet man, and I'll dog ye.*
> *Love my love, sweet man, and I'll hog ye.*
> *Love, love, love me,*
> *Love my dog.*

He smilingly stands at position A.
The Modern Contraption moves from the Forest and jostles.
A door opens, insucks him. He hangs on a strap.
It moves him to B, clanging,
Ejects him, vanishes.

> *Miss, it am a mess but remember*
> *You have a broom*
> *And I have a broom*
> *And we have from now till the 7th of November*

The Contraption returns, reinsucks, moves him back to A,
Ejects him, vanishes. He begins to feel faint.
In the back of his mind like a toy on a shelf he sees fulfillment
    though he is unfulfilled.
He imagines that he is well and vigorous
    though he is deathly ill.

He believes that the welfare of his family, his country and himself
Is contingent upon his continuing what he is doing
        though he is a loss leader.
He has faith in the President and the Congress and the Federal
        Agencies and dislikes shit and eats it.
And the songs keep playing.

                    "Poor man!"

The words come from a tree. Caressing.
A blonde alights from the tree and picks him up gently
And carries him off to her digs and strips him and bathes him.
He curls at her breast, she swings him up on her
And guides him and holds him
And strokes him when he is done and watches him sleep,
Poor dear.
So he wakes and makes for his clothes but she is upon him
And twists his poor arms behind him
And as he cries out in his pain she twists his arms harder
Until he gasps in extremity "Who art thou?" and she hisseth swiftly
"The media!"
And in the bed throweth him fiercely.

        *   *   *

We jump forward.

It is late afternoon in the forest. Every tree is in bankruptcy.
Every leaf has a price stamp on it. Every rock is wrapped.
The only free item
Is evening.
            It is coming.
                        Our hero awaits it.
Yup, the old son of a bitch will sit in a hole

                            and wait.
He won't die easy.
He'll frequent the lobbies of hospitals filling out forms.
His heart will be cleaned and oiled each year, glands repacked
And he'll sit there.

But now it is late afternoon. He is smiling in sufferance.
Released by his lady till supper he strolls in the meadow
Alone
With what she has oft-times told him
Are his own thoughts.
His spirit floats.
Keeoo, kkooee, goes the meadowlark.
The grass ripples.
His senses quicken.

That he should see a rock with his own eyes,
Feel a branch's sting,
Stand alone where the trees begin
And be witness to dark. Like a movie almost.

Perhaps he is not a highly sensitive organism
But he might have made a good field bird or small rodent
Aware of immediate meanings, a learner from rock
                                            but for the lady.
For a moment he stands in his pride, his freedom,
Then speaks:

"I am a bagful of sounds.
Keeoo, kkooee.
It is my conviction
That no man should be deprived of the right to vote.
I firmly believe
That to have great poets one must have great audiences too.
There is no shadow of a doubt in my mind
That we must make the plain facts of sex known to our youngsters.
And make no bones about it,
The most precious asset our dear country has is free speech.
Keeoo, kkooee."

And deep in the forest Ralph Waldo Emerson whispers that the secret
    of civilization is cumulative power

Neglecting to mention that civilization accumulates junk.

And deeper still in the forest the Lord God says to Noah,
    "I plan to let it rain for forty days and forty nights
    and get rid of the junk!"

But Noah says, "Then this is a critical time in human history
    and I bear a grave responsibility for future generations."

And the Lord God says, "It ain't a-gonna work."

    *   *   *

If the truth exists
It exists in the senses

It exists in the tree
And the vision of tree

It exists in the rock
And the knowledge of rock

And the love of rock
And the fear of rock

If the truth exists
It exists in the looking

And the knowledge of looking
And the silence of looking

It exists in the silence
Which is also saying

It exists in the cognizance
Of the silence

So let the tree speak
And the rock

The new leaf
And the brown leaf

The sandstone
And the granite

Let them speak
Let them all speak

Let them keep speaking

And *let* the man listen
That he may speak

Money

Have you heard the bad news?

— the eighteen percenters have fallen on hard times
Their computers are asking time-and-a-half for overtime

So sad

The IRS crooks are stealing from the installment-plan crooks
And the banker crooks
And the conglomerate crooks

Where to get money?

After all
           to be in the business of money means one should have some

But the tax people want at least half
And the eighteen percenters want at least twice what they're getting
And the conglomerate crooks want New York Chicago LA

Which makes it real rough in the money game

But as for those who are not in the money game
                                        well
They keep complaining

They are the ones who supply the work and the goods
That produce money

Don't they know that if they want money they should be *in* money?

— the best information says they will be finally flat
In a couple of months

Down to their mortgaged drawers
Borrowing on the borrowing
Selling old clip-pins and souls
Loss leaders

Which wd be fine if only the crooks of the public
Or the crooks of the private
Sector wd feed them

          but which?

Or would it be fine?

This is an old tragedy in America now pushing the last act
Never before have our aspirations for the common citizen
      been more remote
Never before has the capitalist pit as described by the socialists
      been nearer

We are on the edge

Yet it is agreed by everyone in any position of power (which is money)
That the business of the country is money
That there need be nothing left for the artisan (that sentimental
      fragment out of an old novel)
Nothing left for the worker the clerk the teacher (those modern
      anomalies)
Nothing for the salaried the waged

It is agreed that the proceeds of honest work may be should be will be
      eaten up by "overhead"

Which is indeed over head
               it hangs over
                        it sucks up

Until there is nothing left
               nothing

But the misery of penury for the 99% who are not in money
And the misery of the national soul mired in money

For make no mistake the money game as now played smells
In the private sector
In the public sector
In the Congress and the White House
In the state capitals the city halls
And smells beyond smelling where the cartoon capitalists
Hang out fat as ever taking their cut

It is robbery it is stealing it is theft
It is taking away the earnings of labor
And giving to those who do not labor
                              except as thieves labor
Modern thieves with computers

Marx was right Shaw was right
Name all the old radicals they were right

            but where are the new radicals?
            the new liberals?
            reformers by any label?

— they are writing books about woodsy communes
Picketing for women's lib
Telling us not to eat meat smoke obey teacher
Searching the back alleys for millennia
While the money men gobble

What is this anyway
                  (oh America)?

Get wise

Get the crooks where they are
                        see!
                              they are in
MONEY

Abominable Snowman

The great the abominable snowman has been thinking
He has been looking down with his abominable green eyes
     on the green valley
And now he is putting his abominable paws on
And his abominable fur
And his abominable teeth
He is packing his abominable duffel with ice and snow
And now lifting it to his shoulders and starting slowly
Down the long slope

Down
Out of the whiteness and the gray rock
To trees fields warmth
And now unto people
            the suburbs
The houses in neatly curved rows the wives making toast

He is there now
He is standing abominably on a lawn pushing snow down a chimney
Why is the toast so cold? wonders the wife
The baby blue?
         He moves next door
He knocks he walks through the wall he frosts the TV screen
And leaves as he came nipping violets by the driveway

The suburb is whitening
Starting to look abominable
He is pleased with himself he is doing a good day's work
(He smiles and stiffens a goldfish)
A reporter alights from a snowmobile
              Mr Snowman
Is what you are doing part of a long range plan?
                  Certainly not
I do what I do when I do it I like to express myself

Ode to New York

Let me not be unfair Lord to New York that sink that sewer
Where the best the worst and the middle
Of our land and all others go in their days of hope to be made over
Into granite careerists
Let me not be unfair to that town whose residents
Not content to subside in their own stench
Drag down the heavens let me not be unfair because I have known
An incorruptible New Yorker (he was a saint)
Also NY has produced at least three books
Two plays
A dozen fine dresses meals shirts taxidrivers
Not to mention Jack (Steve?) Brodie
And Mayor LaGuardia why should it matter
That the rest is garbage?
                              No let me be fair
And mention wonders like East 9th Street
Why should anybody care that NY is 2/3 of our country's ills
(And Washington 1/3, and Muncie Dallas Birmingham and LA the rest)
When it has crooks so rich and powerful that when they drive to town
They can park?
Let us not forget that TV is in New York and
              the worst slums
           the largest fortunes
         the most essential inhumanity
Since Nero or maybe Attila as well as
Hospitals that admit no patient without a $300 deposit
                              if I were a local
I'd take the express to Rahway but let me just say
That I don't like New York much
All that corrupt stone
All those dishonest girders decadent manholes diseased telephones
New York reminds me of when I had jaundice
New York is sick in the inner soul

Of its gut but we'll be dead of it
Before it is and so New York
You wonderful fun town
Who inspireth my animus
And leadeth two hundred million other Americans to wish they had not
  been born under the spell of free enterprise but in a Martian
  restroom
              New York
I know that when I speak of you I speak of me
I speak of us
I speak of selves who resolved at the age of four to convert themselves
  into currency
Because at the age of four they (I, we) had already learned
That no food clothing housing
Existed other than currency
And no faith hope charity
Other than currency
              good waterproof dollars
And if there were labor that could not be turned into currency
They (I, we) knew not to do it
And if there were thoughts that could not be turned into currency
They (I, we) knew not to have them

So here we are in the latter day of our wisdom
Yesterday sweetness and light reached a new low
In heavy trading
Even porn is in trouble
              what can be done?
In a decade a dozen of our holiest ones
Will own the island
But rats will be running the island

In a decade not a minute of a working man's day will belong to a
  working man
All subway riders will pay dues to the Limousine Club

Rats will be running the island
There is no surer route to the grave than through NY

And all American routes go through NY
NY lurks in the corners of our churches paintings novels
NY infests our playing fields newspapers trade unions
There is not a square foot of American sidewalk without the mark of
      a NY entrepreneur
Wherever you drive he will cut in front of you
                    he will get there first

Rats on the island
Ravenous rats
Bred by the banks and the stock exchange
Fed by the eighteen percenters
World that will end
But when?

Lord
       you have sent us prophets
They have prattled about revolution and pocketed the proceeds
They have made it
              by an infallible law of New York
In direct proportion to the extravagance and falsehood of their
      announced visions
They have built the hysteria of constant and drastic social change
      into each breakfast
They have taught our children how to stop war on Monday poverty on
      Tuesday racism on Wednesday sexism on Thursday and final
      exams on Friday

Yet nothing changes

And wherever one drives the prophets are out in front
                  they get there first

Rats on the island

Oh New York let me be fair you hell town
I was born to the north of you have lived to the west of you
I have sneaked up on you by land air and sea and been robbed in
      your clip joints

I have left you hundreds of times in the dream that I *could*
Leave you
        but always you sit there
Sinking
      my dearest my sweet
Would you buy these woids?

Foxy Loxy's Christmas Happiness

Just before chicken licken, henny penny, turkey lurkey, ducky wucky and goosey loosey started out for foxy loxy's house on their way to tell the king of the sky's declension,

A poet-knowit, a philosopher-wosopher and a two-legged opportunist joined them in a flurry of excitement to confirm chicken licken's original discovery:

Not only was the sky falling but the ocean was rising and civilization was approaching its end out near the old Carnegie library.

There was no time to lose and chicken licken's prescience was to be commended, but was the king the right person to inform of impendings?

Who was the king anyway? Had anyone seen him? How long had it been since his majesty had placed his seal of approval on a new toothpaste?

At least in the opinion of the newcomers the king was not the commanding personage he had been in the old days,

So it was likely that when he was told that the sky was falling, the ocean rising and civilization approaching its end out near the old Carnegie library, he would simply write a book about it, one of those fashionable new doomsday books,

Which is exactly what poet-knowit, philosopher-wosopher and the two-legged opportunist were themselves projecting already,

Except that *they* wanted to do not a doomsday book but a big, beautiful, happy *anti*-doomsday book in prose and poetry with pages and pages of illustrations for the Christmas trade.

Why then shouldn't chicken licken, henny penny, turkey lurkey, ducky wucky and goosey loosey join them (it would be a sort of love-in) and they'd all do an anthology?

Well! An anthology sounded just fine to chicken licken, henny penny, turkey lurkey, ducky wucky and goosey loosey though they had never been proximate to one.

All they wished to ascertain was: would an anthology be big enough and strong enough to effectively keep the sky from falling, the ocean from rising and civilization from coming to an end?

Out near the Carnegie library?

Well, said the poet-knowit, he wasn't sure but he thought so.

The philosopher-wosopher wasn't sure either, but he thought so.

The two-legged opportunist was sure. He knew so.

He said there was no question of failure so long as they put a bright cover on it, and gave it a snappy title, and commissioned an introduction to it by some authority on the liberated sex life, or Charles Reich, or Timothy Leary, or maybe —

Pollyanna? asked chicken licken.

Mary Baker Eddy? asked ducky wucky.

Jean-Jacques Rousseau? asked turkey lurkey.

Bruce Barton? asked goosey loosey.

Isadora Duncan's brother? asked henny penny.

The two-legged opportunist frowned and said that perhaps an introduction was not necessary so long as the cover was terribly bright and the title snappy.

Then let us, said henny penny happily, betake ourselves swiftly to foxy loxy's delightful Georgian town house and ask him to provide us with a title snappy.

And chicken licken, turkey lurkey, ducky wucky, goosey loosey, poet-knowit, philosopher-wosopher and the two-legged opportunist agreed. It would be a sort of love-in!

Ah, but when at last these earnest entrepreneurs knocked eagerly at the door of foxy loxy's delightful Georgian town house out near the old Carnegie library,

And when at last foxy loxy himself welcomed them into the gracious dining room and sat them down before the roaring fire and asked them what service he could provide them that would be commensurate with their deservings,

Suddenly chicken licken began to feel the sky falling faster,

And suddenly henny penny and the others also began to feel the sky falling faster, not to mention the sea rising and civilization ending pronto.

— So doom came to its day just before dinner and well before Christmas for chicken licken, henny penny, turkey lurkey, goosey loosey and ducky wucky as well as for poet-knowit, philosopher-wosopher and the two-legged opportunist, in a delightful Georgian town house out near the old Carnegie library;

And foxy loxy smiled after his good dinner and said to his good wife that since he had always hated those overpriced Christmas books it was a joy to him to be able to play in this instance the role of the sky and the sea.

The Wolf Again

Surely you remember, my darling, how Mrs Pig sent her three little
    pigs out into the big world to make their fortunes —

For this story appears in your big red book and your
    little yellow book —

And how the first little pig made his house of straw, and what
    happened to him,

And how the second little pig made his house of sticks, and what
    happened to him;

And you remember how the industrious third little pig refused to
    make the mistake of his siblings, and built his house of brick,

So that when the hungry capitalist wolf came huffing and puffing to
    the sturdy brick house

He signally failed to do what he had done to the peasantry and the
    lumpenproletariat,

But slowly and angrily worked himself up into climbing the roof of
    the third pig's house to descend the chimney.

Of course we both know what the shrewd pig had been doing in the
    meantime.

He had been boiling water.

Nowhere in Marx and Engels so far as I know, or even in the later
    writings of the anarcho-syndicalists, is there any suggestion
    that the revolutionary should boil water.

It has instead been the traditional assumption that at the crucial moment the revolutionary will step *out* of his house and attack the wolf.

Right here in this little story we find a unique insight into wolf psychology:

The wolf *had* to descend the chimney.

So the pig boiled water.

Now in the version of the story that you read in your big red book,

The wolf was cooked in the boiling water and eaten by the pig;

But in the version in your little yellow book he jumped out of the water, ran away and was never seen again.

When you are older you will discover that the author of the yellow book took the story from the red book but changed the ending so that you would sleep at night.

When you are older you will also learn of a curious modification produced by the CIA in which the wolf jumps out of the boiling water and eats the third little pig.

But I think you should know now that none of these stories is the true story.

In the true story the wolf, having been terribly burned by the boiling water, leaps from the pot and has his burns cared for by the third little pig;

And the pig and the wolf together then have an all-night psychological "encounter" in which the wolf admits

to his evil ways and confesses to the pig that he
had planned not only to eat him but to use his skin for
capitalist wallets,

And the pig acknowledges that he had some sick-sick plans too, such
as going to bed with the wolf while the wolf was convalescing;

And both as a result come to understand the important things
to understand,

Which are that the big bad wolf is not a big bad wolf but a
misunderstood wolf,

And the good industrious third pig is not a good industrious pig but
an anal and driven pig,

And both need therapy.

So they shake hands.

And apply for a joint grant.

Inventory

To pass through the season of loss and emerge with a good suit
Is to thank God
And take inventory.

The season of waiting is slow.
The clouds hang listlessly.

Where the path bends into the woods
From the meadow
The light is a half light,
And one looks to the north to the hills,
Which are blue.
I will carry the meadow view
Back to the city.

But the woods are close.
They crowd in officiously,
Shutting the heavens out.
One sits in the sullenness
With spiders.

I think that before I die I would like to live
In my good suit
In the meadow.

By My Window

I sit by my window.
I watch the woods.
Now whether it be that I watch the woods
More than the woods watch me
Is a matter for great philosophers, but I know this:
It is not the quarreling finches that spy on me,
Nor my attic squirrel,
Nor any other familiar, not even the great crow
Who struts by —
I see them all in their busyness, they know me not
If I thunder not —
Yet I feel a presence.

I sit at my window.

It must be a presence I know not.
Yet must it not also be someone I know with such intimacy
That I know of his knowing?
It must be myself, then, my very own godliness
Skipping from tree to tree,
God of the wood set aprowl
By me. Me!

I sit at my window.

Mrs Benedict

Oh where are you now Mrs Benedict?
The last time I heard your voice over the phone
I was a child and you were drunk but orderly
And I called mother
                       that you and she could talk
Until I was grown

Talk talk
About nothing that I can remember
Or you could remember
Talk slowly brokenly angrily and without respite

As the years filled with bottles

Where are you now? Where have you taken your permanent bun?
Mother is dead father is dead I sit here old and silent
But somewhere you are still saying
                      something not to remember

On Looking Through a Photo Album
(Of Viet Cong Prisoners)

These pictures show us a ragged, un-uniformed enemy,
Many too young to shave but with trim haircuts,
Many too old to fight but strong in defiance,
Many frightened, hurt, dazed,
Many despairing,
Some squatting numb and expressionless,
Some dead.

Their captors surround them in big boots.

Note that most of the faces are looking off stage;
They see something unpleasant approaching.
But in this one the dog is too tired to look,
And the woman in front is done looking.
She has seen it, whatever it is, and turned off;
                                        her eyes
Are not focussed; she dreams
                        of no mortgage foreclosure,
                        of no missing relief check.

And here is one of mother and child beside stretcher,
Looking at corpse,
Presumably daddy.

And one of a tall American sergeant with scholarly glasses
Holding foe by scruff of neck.

Then there are pictures of blindfolded females,
And slim males with their heads in sandbags, their hands tied behind
        them,
And fierce youths plotting against us,
And graybeards with sealed lips.

All with tags on them.

I am American, middle-aged, male, with college degree.
I have been to war, I have studied war.
I know war to be part of man, death part of war,
And cruelty, deprivation, slaughter of innocents
Part,
Visited on both sides.

Yet I am sold out to this enemy; I like his small ears.
I am struck by his wide forehead, his high cheekbones.
His suppleness pleases me, and his spirit.
When I look at the gun at his chest, the knife at his bowels,
I fear for him.
When I see him hung by the heels I am sick.
The griefs that I find in his wrinkles, his patience in crossed legs,
The sullen undauntedness issuing from him
Swamp me with traitorous feeling.
Don't I know that this is a war? that this is the enemy?

The Washington Ragtime After-Election Gloom-Doom Stomp (1972)

I'd sing the nobody's hometown blues if I knew the tune
Sing the nobody's hometown blues if I knew the tune
In the very blue-est blues town
The ain't nobody home town
Where I sit and watch the cold come down

                                    down

Sit and watch the cold come down

                yeah
                    cat and dog
              dig that

I'd blow this town away if I had a fan
Blow this town away if I had a fan
Town for vulture and ashcan
Bad town yeah man
Where I sit and watch the bad go on

                              on

Sit and watch the bad go on

                zowie
                    zip zap
              boolah

But I'm stuck right in this town for four sad more
Stuck right in this town for four sad more
All stuck and sad and sore
Contemplating four
More of what we didn't need one more

                                  more

Didn't need one sad bad little more

                cut

Oh There You Are!

China oh there you are hello how are you all?
How is your chow mein? ping pong? Great Wall?

And Russia dear Russia hi there you lovely vodka bear
How is your Tea Room? your Party? your Red Square?

And hail Poland all hail your sausages and bran
And hail our friend and teammate brave Iran

             (hi Shah)

Hail and it was swell of us to drop in and confer
Swell of us to bring you peace and Kissinger

And so upon departure we thank you from our heart
For the caviar and pandae and a la carte

We leave you

               ciao

Salute you

               ugh

And head back to carry on the way we always do

OM
    bomb bomb
           OM

Science Fiction

From my city bed in the dawn I see a raccoon
On my neighbor's roof.
He walks along in his wisdom in the gutter
And passes from view
On his way to his striped spaceship to take his disguise off
And return to Mars as himself, a Martian
Raccoon.

Eat-mit-Fingah Shaggy

I sink we shd eat mit fingah.
I sink we shd gobble gobble mit big fat puss on silvah plattah.
I sink we shd burp ze Stars und Stripes forevah,
Und screech und hollah,
Also makem love in dirty underwah.
I sink we shd wuk und wuk to bring utopah,
But nevah be too nize mit mannuh.
Might spoilem.
Might makem sink ze kulchah boojwah,
Und a manifestation of the decadence of the western capitalist poobah.
Therefah for openah
I sink we all go pow each othah
Und yellem yah! bah!
Etceterah.

Frankie and Johnnie Revisited

Frankie and Johnnie certainly had a nice hook-up
(Frankie was a girl)
For many years in outer Saskatchewan ten miles north of Teacup
Where they ran a still
And had a double bed that they made creak
At ten o'clock each Saturday night after the whiskey
Had stopped dripping for the week.

Everybody in town thought they were a perfect pair
And if you had asked Johnnie to run for alderman he would have said
    yes and he would have won
And if you had asked Frankie where she would have lived if she could
    have gone anywhere
She would have said ten miles north of Teacup because that was where
    her wants were none.
Yes theirs was a glorious interpersonal relationship for many and
    many a year
And it might still be relating if Johnnie had not found another and
    somewhat less settled dear

Named Alice Frankie was furious.
She was willing to put up with frostbitten fingers and chapped lips
And even wolves at the door if they weren't curious
But another woman relating, especially one named Alice,
Unhinged her so that she took of the whiskey nips
And shot her Johnnie and was thereupon hung henceforth
And went off to hell but that wasn't bad after all because persons
    there talked of love not interpersonal relationships.
Also it was only ten miles further north.

For the Life of Him and Her

For the life of her she couldn't decide what to wear to the party.
All those clothes in the closet and not a thing to wear.
Nothing to wear, nothing wearable to a party,
Nothing at all in the closet for a girl to wear.

For the life of him he couldn't imagine what she was doing up there.
She had been messing around in that closet for at least an hour,
Trying on this, trying on that, trying on all those clothes up there,
So that they were already late for the party by at least an hour.

If only he wouldn't stand around down in the hall,
She could get herself dressed for the party, she knew she
    could somehow,
But he made her so nervous, he was so nervous there in the hall
That she didn't think they would get to the party anyhow.

He didn't want to go to the party anyhow,
And he didn't want to stand and stand in the hall,
But he didn't want to tell her he didn't want to go anyhow.
He just didn't want to, that's all.

Old Poems
1945-1970

The Elm City

The hard yellow reversible wicker seats
Sit in my mind's warm eye varnished row on row
In the old yellow childhood trolley
At the end of the line at Cliff Street where the conductor
Swings the big wooden knob on the tall control box
Clangs the dishpan bell and we wander off

To tiptoe on stones and look up at bones in cases
In the cold old stone and bone of the Peabody Museum
Where the dinosaur and the mastodon stare us down
And the Esquimaux and the Indians stare us down

In New Haven
The Elm City

I left that town long ago for war and folly
Phylogeny rolled to a stop at the old Peabody
I still hear the dishpan bell of the yellow trolley

Clamming

I go digging for clams once every two or three years
Just to keep my hand in (I usually cut it),
And whenever I do so I tell the same story
Of how at the age of four I was trapped by the tide
As I clammed a sandbar. It's no story at all
But I tell it and tell it; it serves my small lust
To be thought of as someone who's lived.
I've a war too to fall back on, and some years of flying,
As well as a high quota of drunken parties,
A wife and children; but somehow the clamming thing
Gives me an image of me that soothes my psyche
Like none of the louder events: me helpless,
Alone with my sandpail,
As fate in the form of soupy Long Island Sound
Comes stalking me.

I've a son now at that age.
He's spoiled, he's been sickly.
He's handsome and bright, affectionate and demanding.
I think of the tides when I look at him.
I'd have him alone and sea-girt, poor little boy.

The self, what a brute it is. It wants, wants.
It will not let go of its even most fictional grandeur
But must grope, grope down in the muck of its past
For some little squirting life and bring it up tenderly
To the lo and behold of death, that it may weep
And pass on the weeping, keep the thing going.

                Son, when you clam,
Watch out for the tides and take care of yourself,
Yet no great care,

Lest you care too much and brag of the caring
And bore your best friends and inhibit your children and sicken
At last into opera on somebody's sandbar. Son, when you clam,
Clam.

The Philadelphia Vireo

". . . anyone unable to tell a Vireo from a Warbler is
hardly ready to recognize this species." — *A Field
Guide to the Birds* by Roger Tory Peterson

One can't do much in these woods without a bird book.
Right on my porch sits a light-breasted thing I name phoebe,
      building a nest;
And the pines by the house are held by a reddish-brown thrush and his
      reddish-brown mate,
Along with the smallest bird on the place, some warbler or finch,
Who struts down below on the needles on match-stick legs.
Far out and high I hear what I think is mocking bird; then there
      are crows,
Robins, jays, a few pheasants, what-all. I march up and down with
      my bird book, scholarly,
Interested in the variety of sounds and shapes,
Amused by my own insufficiencies as stalker of wild life,
But otherwise little disposed to be moved: to commune, to identify.

Back at the house I page through an angry Tolstoi berating the Greeks
For beguiling the artless Christians with pre-Christian nudes.
I close Tolstoi. He should have sniped at the birds too while
      he was at it,
Little pagans, for putting so many poets in bushes with bird books.
It's a bad day and I feel like a fool out here with these chirpers,
And now I'm writing these lines, dissonant things, and
      thinking bird things,
Because I'm a professional bird and am programmed to sing.
So I sing: chrrrk, chrrrk.

But why should I run down the birds? They have energy, they
      are strange.
There is wonder in energy, strangeness. Art needs that, man
      needs that,

And I seem to be in these woods for that, though writing a man-book.
So I say to my phoebe, the one on the porch, the builder,
Who is flying in sticks to her nest like a drunken west wind: bird,
Man thinks, though he thinks too much for all he knows of thee,
    well of thee.

Spring, Etc.

And now at last I come to it: spring,
Spring with his shoures sote,
Shoures of snowe stille in Minnesota
But spring all the same, starting all over
All of those worthy projects in grass and clover
That somehow got tabled last October.

Spring in the trees and gardens, spring in the mind,
Spring in the fields and rivers, spring in the blood,
Spring, spring, spring, and then again spring,
Wet, warm, bright, green, good.

So now at last I come to it,
Long long overdue,
Come to it late by bobsled and skate, but come
To it, by golly and gum!
To it! Tu-whit, tu-who!

The High School Band in September

On warm days in September the high school band
Is up with the birds and marches along our street,
Boom boom,
To a field where it goes boom boom until eight forty-five
When it marches, as in the old rhyme, back, boom boom,
To its study halls, leaving our street
Empty except for the leaves that descend to no drum
And lie still.
In September
A great many high school bands beat a great many drums,
And the silences after their partings are very deep.

Jackson in Winter

"Solid, Jackson!"
— Louis Armstrong

Darkness comes early, stays late
In my winter country; the frost
Goes four feet down; trees are like sticks.
A light snow lingers
For a month or two, getting dirty. I write every day
But throw much away.

My third book will appear in the spring, a small book,
A slight book,
Containing no plays or long narrative poems,
Borrowing hardly at all from the middle ages,
Making few affirmations, avoiding inversions,
Using iambics distrustfully, favoring lines
Of odd lengths and irony.
                              I am forty.
I seem to know the dimensions of what I can do
And the season to do it in.
Give me a few more winters like this one, and spring —
Or the thought of spring —
Will cease to be a disturbance and I'll be
Solid Jackson.

The Seven Days

Introduction

On the last day of the old world I stretched
Out my bones like a fossil fathoms down
And bade time's leavings cover me layer on layer
And death sweep over, over me in her sea gown.

On the first day of the new world I stood
On a porch on a hill in the dark with a pencil
And bade there be light in the east and took my pencil
With me into the light and set to brood.

On First Looking at Crotched Mountain, New Hampshire

Take from my thoughts those shells paleozoic.
No petrified foraminifer yet am I.
Leave the siftings stiffen in their sea bed.
To live in the past, says this old saw, is to die.

Let a sun, now, be born. Let a mountain be folded.
And now let the sun climb up and inquisitively peer
Over at me as I birth and eyes open
To a new landscape there, a new seer here.

I call these pines pines, this ivy poison.
I call all those small birds finches, that big one crow.
But what will I call that mountain? Crotched? Absurd.
Yet Crotched it is. I say so, and I know.

Praise be to me (not God; Him I haven't spoke yet)
For this new day. May I now breakfast beget.

On First Knowing God

At breakfast I had french toast
(I nomenclate thee french toast)
And drank several cups of coffee
(This will soon be arithmetic)
And came back to my bathroom
And emptied my new bowels
And said to the pines, Who is God?

The wind was up, the pines
Noisy but recondite.
An ant crawled up my shirt.
I took off my shirt and baked,
And looked at Mount Crotched and dozed.
Who was to tell me, tell me?
Not the leaves, not the pines,
Not the sun, not the ant.
Had I made nothing would speak to me?
I went to the finch in the leaves
And said, Someone must say.
But he flew away.

How about you, robin,
You on the stump?
But the robin zipped to the underbrush
And a hush fell on the brush
And I understood as I stood
Bare to the waist on a stone
That the robin had known.
The stone upheld me.

To my porch then did I walk
And did to the mountain cry,
God, God am I.

The Second Day

On the second day of creation
I rose again with the sun
And walked up and down the earth —
I, the One.

But I heard the pert jay
And saw the drooped birch
And stubbed the stone.
Whose was this church?

So I came cold to my cabin
And lighted a Sterno can
And drank tea at my desk,
Idle, a man.

And I knew then how soon
Begetting turns to begot
And wondered who, from the first day,
Would choose God's lot.

Lament

But who is he, said the god, said the man, who is choosing?
The bird and the poem take shape, and the act of shaping
Is a dying into the shaping, the bird's god shriveling
To a bird, the poem's to a poem. From the heavens
The earth's begetters, gods and poets, straggle

Down to that earth, makers unmade,
And knock at the earth's doors, and go to their trade.

And their trade, said the god, said the man, the
     god-part done,
Is to live by their bond to what was once their sun,
Watching the days sift down to the great sea bed,
Waiting, those dead gods, to be dead.

VI

The Third Day

There was no third sunrise.
Crotched was smoked up.
I stayed inside at the fire, pared my toenails,
Looked at the veins in my legs, felt the bones' nearness.

The cabin was dark, the chairs sulky, gray the windows.
The whole had the look of a party that didn't come off
Because somebody put all the liquor and talk in a drawer
And said, Sit there; Be sad; Concentrate.

'Twas a meditative goddam place,
The books stacked in a corner reading themselves,
And the wooden lists on the walls of writers, composers,
Gods who had been there before me, now just hanging there,
And the big table with claw feet, poised by the jungle (rug)
Ready to rip something up, maybe a poet,
And prove Darwin. I did push-ups,
But the younger poet was getting too old for push-ups;
So I went outside and the sun was out of the smoke now,
And the birds and the bugs were at it again, world
Without end; so I went to breakfast.

Tell me the story of Job, Mom, the story of Job.
Was he the one with the big, scratchy bathrobe?

Or was he the man with the locusts? Mom, tell me.
I want to hear about somebody like me.

Breakfast was poached eggs and a good bit of talk,
And the toaster popped up and down and the artists
      looked nervous.
I thought of all of them thinking like me of trudging
Each back to his god-hole after the coffee,
Then sitting awhile on the toilet then tidying this up
And that up,
And smoking like mad and circling the desk like a hawk
Coming in with care on a smelly carcass. Gods?
I went back and did all that.

What is the name of that Indian in Cooper
Who walks through the primeval forest like a ghost?
Teach me the lore of silence, how to make it
Creepily through the thicket
On dry twigs, eating dry toast.

I went and sat like a stump in the nine a.m. sun,
On the lee side, looking south at a different parnassus,
Hazy, a sketch of mountain that could be cloud,
And I wondered if the gods there were also dead.

VII

Lament

Out there beyond the porch where my god-country
Starts to get dense and godly,
I am.
That brown thrush is me,
Blasting it out in the woods, Omar Khayyám.

In the sun, nude, oozing out to the spruces,
Moss, fat beetles, stumps, boulders
I lie.

Pretty soon I'll be immanent in the firmament
With here a bit, there a bit, everywhere a bit-bit, of me
        right by.

But when the lugs from the heavenly poetry society
Gathering up their far-flung warbler blokes
To my woods come,
They won't find much but some undone verse, some old smokes,
And an empty chair by a desk in an empty room.

VIII

The Fourth Day

I had just one match.
I lighted the Sterno with it,
And a cigaret, and made coffee,
And craftily shut the Sterno down to a thin flame,
And went to the desk and smoked the cigaret,
And finished the coffee, made busy and reached for a cigaret,
And went to the Sterno flame: out.

With the matches a mile away and no other god up,
My old trivial life swept in like a mist.
I fretted an hour, paced, kept looking for matches,
Then padded early to breakfast, found matches.

Somebody was impelled, over her poached egg,
To play out with gestures the drama of climbing the Matterhorn.
I backed out away from that, back to the cabin,
And smoked, smoked. The mountains were hidden
The trees stood stony, a thousand strong; so the shrubs.
And the grass, even the grass, each frail dry blade
Was fixed as if behind glass with a card in front of it:
"Of the order *Graminae*."

Was this the Peabody Museum? Where was the guard?
I remembered there a wax Indian, loincloth and tomahawk,

'Twas I, but now wearing shorts, waving a cigaret.
What would *my* card say?

—"Of the order *Americanus parnassianus;*
Ranged Narrowly;
Is Extinct though still Living near Crotched Mountain
Quietly."

IX

The Fifth Day

On the fifth day the first god made great whales
And creeping things.
I got up late with a head and barely made breakfast
And sat in my cabin still fuzzy from too much beer,
Wondering what I was doing there.
The mountains were clear, the air had a rinsed look,
But the land was dry, unchanged. I was still in the museum.
My wife and children were half a country away.
The sun kept tearing around in the empty sky.
I was forty-five. I was old. I wanted to cry.

X

The Sixth Day

On the sixth day, after coffee, I made man.
I made him hairy, tan, middle-aged, arrogant.
I gave him warts, colds, wit, phobias, woman.
I put books in his hands and taught him to drive, dance,
Lie with woman.
I put him out in the sun under Crotched Mountain,
And I looked at him.

He was well-made, would get on.
He would sleep poorly at night as he got older,

77

Would forget people's names, misquote things, drink too much,
Rage at woman at breakfast, lose keys.
With bankers he'd be ill at ease.

But he'd work hard and make money and pay his taxes
And vote for the school bond issue and love woman
And take children to zoos and wear tweeds.
He was well-made.

I looked at him.
He was sitting out on the steps of the cabin in shorts.
He had no mark on him.
His body was firm. He was muscular. His hair was still black.
Yet the eyes, and mouth, and flesh of the cheeks and forehead
Were old. He looked out across ages, like a saurian.

What had I made?

I went in the cabin and worked, but could only think of him.
The afternoon came on, no wind, no motion.
Whatever I did he was there. The hours passed,
And I wrote these words and evening crept in the cabin,
And a hush came over things and the sky darkened
And I sat in the cabin with him and he slept.

I watched him sleep.
At last I got up and left, left the cabin to him.

XI

The Seventh Day and Conclusion

There, then, was the world. The man surveyed it.
He doubted it was his duty to call it good.
He knew it to be but a world like any other.
He knew that his god, now resting, had made what he could.

What Was It Like?

What was it like? I can tell you what it was like.
We were sitting and drinking, drinking.
We ticked off all the hatreds of our acquaintance.
We banished the sky from the heavens and it was like death.

And what was death like?
Death, I can tell you now, was like being.
Death was 45, alcoholic, rational,
With the smoke curling up from the fingers, the words from the mouth,
And the wife sitting prim in the corner watching the world end.
Death was all that crap in somebody's living room
On a Saturday night on the circuit with plates in the laps.

We put on our coats and stumbled out to the car
And made it home to the babies and paid the baby sitter
And lay down at last and slept. It was like that.

Song of the Patient Patient

My room overlooks the park.
The trees are like barbed wire.
My keepers are friendly but firm.
I am safe here.

Upright in bed mechanical,
Having bent to the temperature taker,
I await the tray lunch
Cooked by my maker.

My blood is in vats at the lab,
Also my urine.
My pills will appear at three.
X-ray wants me.

Am I deserving? No matter.
In shift serene I give thanks
For roses and mums
And respirator.

Let there be joy amid interns,
Let cashiers dance,
That I may further the work
And look at the park.

The Mind

The mind wears many hats, many different wares.
Like a bird on a spit it turns in its living sleep.
It is quick, slow, open, secret, crammed with
  jokes, prayers.
It knows not what it knows deep.

Yet I have known one kind of mind whose vision
Is steady as the sphinx's, and whose mold
Is rock against all sea and salt and season.
Such a mind, soul, have the old.

They traffic in fixities; they sit in corners sipping.
In the sharp declivities of the times they
  save their breath.
They are more put out by a misplaced tool or letter
Than birth or death.

And when they talk they talk to themselves;
  their rhetoric
Wanders off into privacies where a word
Cares not who hears it, and eloquence
Is a canard.

I know a mind, soul, whose time now leads it
Shoreward to silence.
Not long ago it chattered like half a school,
And bade the desert dance.

The Fall of the House of Usher

It was a big boxy wreck of a house
Owned by a classmate of mine named Rod Usher,
Who lived in the thing with his twin sister.
He was a louse and she was a souse.

While I was visiting them one wet summer, she died.
We buried her,
Or rather we stuck her in a back room for a bit,
    meaning to bury her
When the graveyard dried.

But the weather got wetter.
One night we were both waked by a twister,
Plus a screeching and howling outside that
    turned out to be sister
Up and dying again, making it hard for Rod to
    forget her.

He didn't. He and she died in a heap, and I left
    quick,
Which was lucky since the house fell in right after,

                   Like a ton of brick.

A Teacher

"And gladly wolde he lerne, and gladly teche."

He hated them all one by one but wanted to show them
What was Important and Vital and by God if
They thought they'd never have use for it he was
Sorry as hell for them, that's all, with their genteel
Mercantile Main Street Babbitt
Bourgeois-barbaric faces, they were beyond
Saving, clearly, quite out of reach, and so he
G-rrr
Got up every morning and
G-rrr
Ate his breakfast and
G-rrr
Lumbered off to his eight o'clock
Gladly to teach.

Paul Revere's Ride

Is it one if by land, two if by sea?
Or two if by land? Or what?
What farms, what villages are those to be
Roused from their midnight rut?

Worry, worry, worry. There! A light?
Of course not. But for an empty head
I'd quit this profitless, cold post to plot
The Revolution home in bed.

Yet if the British do, the Tower hunts me down.
Then I mount swiftly; then I fiercely ride,
Bearing fresh news of the infamous Crown
To agitate the countryside.

But if the British do,
I wonder, is it one if by land, or two?

Today

Today is one of those days when I wish I knew everything,
   like the critics.
I need a bit of self-confidence, like the critics.
I wish I knew about Coptic, for example, and Shakti-Yoga.
The critics I read know them, and they say so. I wish I
   could say so.
I want to climb up some big publishing mountain and wear a little
   skullcap and say so: I know.

Confidence, that's what I need — to know —
And would have if I came from California or New York. Or France.
If I came from France I could say such things as, "Art opened its
   eyes on itself at the time of the Renaissance."
If I came from California I could say, "Christianity was short-
   circuited by Constantine."
If I came from New York I could say anything.

I come from Minnesota.
I must get a great big book with all the critics in it
And eat it. One gets so hungry and stupid in Minnesota.

Variations on Being Thirty

The oven is sticky with grease,
And the latch on the broken door to the backyard is broken.
An arm to the sofa is off,
And the new phonograph needles are mixed
With the old phonograph needles.

These are most certainly signs.

The faucet drips in the sink,
And the bulb in the overhead lamp in my bedroom is out.
Six months of *The Times*
Have gathered in heaps in the closet, and neighbor Bates
Is girding himself to demand that I cut my lawn.

That these are signs is as clear as the nose on my face.

Sitting here on the sofa
Watching the ceiling crack and the paint fade,
Watching the rugs gather dust and the doors warp,
Watching the bulbs burn out and the curtains stiffen,
I have been struck, I have been touched, I have been saddened

By instance on top of instance, sign on sign.

The absence of rhyme, for example.
And meter?
And what of the thoughts and feelings? The care, the infinite care?

Instance on top of instance, sign on sign.

I have been sitting here on the broken sofa
Watching the slow decline of second-hand cars,
Watching the slipping of cotton and phonographs,
Watching the West decline.

It Is Not Clear

It is not clear
Where we go from here
Or for that matter
Who we're.

The Self-Made Man

At first he was merely sullen, gentlemen. Growing,
He figured, was gratis;
And if there were someone to thank, very well,
But not much. Later,
Making a pile in the market he put his old mother
To pasture and started to buy things —
Planes, wives, ranches — until he could look
For miles in any direction and see only
His own, very own creations, and thus was led
Into philosophy, where he bred
A phoenix as mascot and climbed onto rostrums,
Saying,
"I am Alpha and so forth. I take the clay
Which is myself, and with my own hands
Mold me as I only may, me me, believe me."

His friends were terribly pleased. They had never
Before known a god, and so they
Crowded around him and asked him to teach them
How to be one. Which he did.
And for six difficult days, like Swedish masseurs,
They molded themselves in his image, and told
    themselves gravely
To multiply and replenish the earth and subdue it.
Which they did.
And on the seventh day, resting, they looked at each other,
And then looked at him and themselves, and were pleased, for lo!
All of them were like him and he was like
Them, and together they
Cut a singular figure as they chanted:
"I am Alpha and so forth. I take the clay

Which is myself, and with my own hands
Mold me as I only may, me me, believe me."

And America prospered.
The corn grew, and the wheat, and all that, and the other God
(Who had been elsewhere)
Returned in due course and looked on the fields and factories
And rejoiced to think he would not in this instance wax wroth —
No flood —
And forthwith went down out of heaven and walked in that land,
Walked in its country lanes and city streets,
And was pleased,
Until he heard snickers behind him and, turning, beheld
A multitude tiptoeing after him snickering, whispering
"Here is one we forgot. Don't he look funny?"

Then, gentlemen,
Then was he wroth? Look at me.
Look at me on this rostrum, note that no lightning
Channels my cheeks.
I speak to you lightly.
I say to you I am a poet, I take the Lord
Here as I need him and mold him to my
Creation, not his, and yet man and beast
Walk on this earth unharmed, and all creeping things
Creep as they crept before, and no whirlwind speaks to me.
And I say to you,
I am Alpha and so forth, and that which I am,
That which I mold from this clay,
Is all the whirlwind there is, or the lightning,
All that commandeth the morning, wingeth the peacock
Draweth the whale from the deep, or maketh
The dust.
And I say to you,
Where in my chatter, where in my banter,
Where, where in this impious figure before you
Is God's wrath?

II

To be like a god, to mold and to hold
Earth as one's private estate,
You must be up and about it
Early and late.

> ". . . was at the office at 7:10 every
> morning."

Start with convictions, be ready to talk
Far into the night
On firming the flesh and the spirit up,
As Polonius might.

> "When I am stripped and manacled . . .
> it is necessary to preserve absolute seren-
> ity of spirit."

Then train, train for action
(With sweatshirts, weights, dark bread,
Steambaths and a notebook
By your bed),

> ". . . he would practice going under wa-
> ter in his own bathtub."

For years, years, and then, primly,
Walking a city street,
Bump some old god, catch him
In mid-air, and meet.

> "Edison sent for him to be his personal
> secretary."

III

In the beginning, gentlemen,
There was a road, icy,
And farmhouses all in a long, sparse line in the snow.
Through this scene I moved in a gray light
For a decade or two, farmhouses passing, fences,
And then came to the main street of a town

Garish with Christmas, and paused for a moment
In front of a crude crêche, but heard no
Sound from the bells, shoppers, passing cars, no
Sound but that of the sea — breakers, shells
Rolling in froth, wind in long grass;
And so I drove on up a slight hill, and the town
Vanished,
And there, icy, as in the beginning,
Was a road,
And farmhouses in a long, sparse line in the snow.

IV

The old god, being grateful, looks into your eyes,
Sees rough diamonds shining there, and buys.
You loosen up a bit, take off your sweatshirt,
Grow sociable and gracious, put your best foot
In the best doors, enter, stay,
Growing more celestial every day.

> "Go to sleep, my little one.
> Soon you'll weigh at least a ton."

And so you settle down, and block by block,
Or line by labored line, or stock by stock,
Build your own new world, and with the vision
Of an old god make provision
For tacking on more world, in case you later
Gauge your greatness to be greater.

> "When his power was firm in electricity,
> he captured gas."

And having done (or started) you look down
On all your works, and beam, and don your crown,
And tell yourself, or have your creatures tell you
What a fine earth yours is, and how well you
Raised this up and put that under,
Stuck to principles and shared your plunder.

For part and parcel of a god's design
Must be to prove to others he's divine.
A horn or two to blow, an ad to print
Will keep your realms intact, your mints aglint,
Until the truth about you, that cruel rope
That tethers you to some mere Alpine slope,
Snaps and you shoot skyward like a prayer,
Propelled by your own prose, your own hot air.

> "My next novel . . . I'm already getting
> gleams for it; I see it as the biggest
> thing I've tackled."

And this is as it should be. You at last
Can leave behind your wormy side, your past,
And having not yet met your future think
You are forever in the pink,
Free in spirit, free in lust to breed a
Christ or Christmas daily with some Leda.

> " 'Now,' he said delightedly, 'I can do any-
> thing I like.' "

v

The mind, gentlemen,
The mind makes music sometimes,
Not words. Images
Dance to this music, passing
Back and forth in a pattern, printing
The same delicate pattern over and over,
So that
A nameless man climbs a nameless hill and descends
And climbs again and descends and his motions are wordless,
And all of that landscape is wordless, fences, trees
Being not what they say but what, speechless, he points at
As he climbs and descends his hill and hears nothing, nothing,
And the sea moans in his ear, and the shells sing,
And the wind in the beach grass whirrs, making this music.

Mary Baker of New Hampshire,
Mary Baker of New Hampshire.
I speak it twice; the rhythm stamps her
Simple Mary of New Hampshire.

What shall I say of Mary? Shall I whine
That she, like Lycid, died before her prime?
(She lived to eighty-nine, then left behind
Three million dollars, and a million of her Mind.)
Or shall I say that she, a shepherdess,
No more the wild Thyme and the Willow may caress?

— No, Coleridge would be better.

Mary Baker of New Hampshire
Lived within her skin
For fifty years, then found her mind
And lived in it, in Lynn.

> "It was decided between them that they
> should go to Lynn, then a town of some
> 30,000 souls, where Mrs. Glover felt that
> the large shoe factory population might
> offer good prospects."

The name she went by then was Glover,
Or Patterson — take your pick —
For she had left two men behind
And was with Eddy thick.

— Where shall I turn? Whose muse will make me ready
To deal with this Mary Baker Eddy?

Leaving Lynn she took her bible
(Having, then, a bible written),
Went to Boston with her bible,

Fed no pigeons on the Common,
Working hard in Boston.

Said the dead she'd bring back life to,
Make the sick and crippled over,
Teach all comers how to conquer
Flesh and body's spirit for a
Flat three hundred.

"She asserted she could restore the dead to life, walk upon water, live without air."

Sent out copies of her bible,
Watched its circulation flourish,
Built a church and called it mother,
Fixed the Lord's Prayer up to suit her,
She no Hiawatha.

"Copies for review were sent . . . with the request to editors that nothing at all be said about the book if the notice could not be laudatory."

— Oh, I must beg your pardon
If I in this cradle rocking
Fall asleep and fail again to
Make my lady's case heroic.

Mary Baker of New Hampshire.
Mary Baker of New Hampshire.

The phrase sticks like a burr.

VII

I spend my winters a thousand miles from the sea.
Images of the beaches and the long grass,
And pools left in the rocks by the tide, and flats

Scattered with driftwood, and shells — all of these
Come to me singing as out of caves, as I
Struggle to rise out of sleep, climbing, descending,
And look out my cold window at the snow.

> "He held directorates in 85 companies,
> he was chairman of 65, president of 11:
> it took three hours to sign his resigna-
> tions."

Images.
These are mine, I say, mine
From the beginning, my beginning, but I
Wonder, if they are mine, why they forever
Fail me? Why are they bare, those flats, those beaches,
Why do they come to me, wordless, singing,
As in the beginning,
The same old childish music as I climb, descend,
And climb again, and age, and find no means
To make them do my bidding;
But only music,
Their music. Why?
                Is it that I
Am a barren god and may not
Say, Let there be warmth, Let there be breeding,
But must dictate only sand and yet more sand, and lay my own
World waste, and look out sadly on it through my window?

> "That was a curious performance, with
> the magician, suave and smiling, forcing
> himself through his exacting repertoire,
> while every gesture and motion was a
> torture."

I do not know.

Gentlemen,
When God looked down on man and saw the wickedness,
He repented and was grieved and said that Noah
And his wife, and two
Of every living thing — one male, one female —
Would alone be spared; and then He sent
The rain to do His bidding, and for forty

Days and nights it rained, destroying
All flesh that moved on earth

> "Samuel Insull wept, Brother Martin wept.
> The lawyers wept . . . there wasn't a dry
> eye in the jury."

Of fowl, of cattle, of every creeping thing,
And of man,
         but the ark

He spared, and when the waters
Sank God came to Noah, saying
Be fruitful; multiply; replenish earth, My
Earth. And thus
Out of the waste, out of the whirlwind,
Up from the desert flats where the water buried
One world, yet another grew and God
Then blessed it.
            But I . . .
Gentlemen . . .

> " 'after fifty years of work,' he said, 'my
> job is gone.' "

Notes: This poem got its start with a sentence in R. W. B. Lewis's book *The American Adam*: "Whitman is an early example . . . of the self-made man, with an undeniable grandeur which is the product of his own manifest sense of having been responsible for his own being." The quotations used in the poem's gloss are from the following sources: *Mrs. Eddy,* by Edwin Franken Dakin; *The Big Money,* by John Dos Passos; *The Lords of Creation,* by Frederick Lewis Allen; *Houdini,* by Harold Kellock; *From Main Street to Stockholm* (Letters of Sinclair Lewis, 1919–1930); and *The Song of Babar.*

The Line of an American Poet

That American poet's future
Was bright because he began
With the know-how of Ford and Chrysler
And the faith of American Can.

He fathomed success's secret
And stuck to his P's & Q's
And urged himself over and over
To produce and produce and produce.

His very first models were cleverly
Built. The market boomed.
Some of the world's most critical
Consumers looked and consumed.

Lines off his line came smoother
And smoother as more and more
Know-how blew in the window
And verses rolled out the door

Until everyone in the market
Knew that his new works were sure
To be just what the country had need of:
Poems uniform, safe and pure.

Alfred Lord Tennyson

"That is all that you will ever make
from poetry." — The Reverend George
Tennyson, upon giving 16-year-old
Alfred half a guinea for some verses

Alfred was a ninny
With his father's half guinea.
He didn't make more
Till he was thirty-four,
And what he got then
Was a gift from the Queen
For having a bit
Of a deficit.

But at fifty, ah,
He lived like a shah
And said to himself,
My name is pelf.
He took a big bite
Of the Isle of Wight,
And though his publisher failed
Fred's fortunes sailed
Up up
With Morgan and Krupp.

So when he died
He had gratified
His heart's dear itch
To be rich, to be rich.
With considerable bother
He had shown his father
You never can tell
What will sell.

A Projection

I wish they would hurry up their trip to Mars,
Those rocket gentlemen.
We have been waiting too long; the fictions of little men
And canals,
And of planting flags and opening markets for beads,
Cheap watches, perfume and plastic jewelry
Begin to be tedious. What we need now
Is the real thing, a thoroughly bang-up voyage
Of discovery.

Led by Admiral Byrd
In the *Nina, Pinta* and *Santa Maria*
With a crew of one hundred experts
In physics, geology, war and creative writing,
The expedition should sail with a five year supply
Of pemmican, Jell-o, Moxie,
Warm woolen socks and jars of Gramma's preserves.

Think of them out there,
An ocean of space before them, using no compass,
Guiding themselves by speculative equations,
Looking,
Looking into the night and thinking now
There are no days, no seasons, time
Is only on watches,
                    and landing on Venus
Through some slight error, bearing

Proclamations of friendship,
Declarations of interstellar faith,
Acknowledgments of American supremacy
And advertising matter.

I wonder,
Out in the pitch of space, having worlds enough,
If the walled-up, balled-up self could from its alley
Sally.
I wish they would make provisions for this,
Those rocket gentlemen.

Lines

Composed upon Reading an Announcement by Civil
Defense Authorities Recommending that I Build a
Bomb Shelter in my Backyard

I remember a dugout we dug in the backyard as children
And closed on top with an old door covered with dirt
And sat in, hour by hour, thoroughly squashed,
But safe, with our chins on our knees, from the world's hurt.
There, as the earth trickled down on us as in an hourglass,
Our mothers called us, called us to come and be fed,
But we would not, could not hear them, possessed as we were
By our self's damp stronghold among the selfless dead.

Now they say willy nilly I must go back
And under the new and terrible rules of romance
Dig yet another hole in which like a child
My adult soul may trifle with circumstance.
But I'll not, no, not do it, not go back
And lie there in that dark under the weight
Of all that earth on that old door for my state.
I know too much to think now that if I creep
From the grown-up's house to the child's house I'll keep.

Still Life

I must explain why it is that at night in my own house,
Even when no one's asleep, I feel I must whisper.
Thoreau and Wordsworth would call it an act of devotion;
Others would call it fright. It is probably
Something of both. In my living room there are matters I'd
    rather not meddle with
Late at night.

I prefer to sit very still on the couch watching
All the dead things of my daytime life —
The furniture and the curtains, the pictures and books —
Come alive,
Not as in some childish fantasy, the chairs dancing,
But with dignity,
The big old rocker presiding over a silent
And solemn assembly of all my craftsmen,
From Picasso and other celebrities gracing my walls
To the local carpenter benched at my slippered feet.

I find these proceedings
Remarkable for their clarity and intelligence, and wish I
    might somehow
Bring into daylight the eloquence, say, of a doorknob.
But always the gathering breaks up; everyone there
Shrinks from the shock of confronting
A cough, a creaking stair.

Love Song

I know not how to speak to thee, girl (damselle?),
Nor how to begin to begin with thee to commune
In all your lazy lingos, oh my America!
Or say to you, honey (light of my life, doll),
That on you I'm sweet.

America, child,
Thou of the silken thighs and purple sagebrush,
How, huh, does it fare with thee?
Art thou Wyoming, Memphis? Yare art thou?
What dost thy lover durst, what idiom suffer
To the apple be
Of thine eye?

Your suitors grow old, old, their lyrics sodden,
And their passions fizz in the soft westering rhetoric,
But you, oh Nik Nak Nookie, Dairie Queene,
From all your Southern Cal to Keep Maine Green,
You still — or so thou tellest me? — mean?

In the Woods (1965)

I sit in the woods of New Hampshire and read of the South.
Nothing new, more murder, more hate, more data on man,
From Mississippi again, that bastion.

My woods are calm, but I keep the radio on.
The northern reporters have all been flying down.
Evil's been trapped, it seems, in some small town.

I sit in my woods in my righteousness and write;
One more reporter-preacher trysts with fate.
Is today *my* day to say to the South, Repent?

Fabre, the great bug man, first proved that reason
Had nothing at all to do with the complex actions
Of bees, ants and the like. Now we in season

Prove the same about us. Now the clocks strike
And we line up as a thousand times before
For the same not black-man white-man, nor south-man north-man, but
  ant-man war.

The Sad Committee Shaggy

In good ole day ze king need no committee.
Was nize.
Him says, them does; him sells, them buys.
Good system.
But then come big push make king one of guys.
So king buy chairs, say me no king me chairman.
So knocked off paradize.

A Day with the Foreign Legion

On one of those days with the Legion
When everyone sticks to sofas and itches and bitches —
A day for gin and bitters and the plague —
Down by Mount Tessala under the plane trees,
Seated at iron tables cursing the country,
Cursing the times and the natives, cursing the drinks,
Cursing the food and the bugs, cursing the Legion,
Were Kim and Bim and all the many brave heroes
Of all the books and plays and poems and movies
The desert serves.
And as they sat at the iron tables cursing the country
Some sergeant or other rushed in from the fort
Gallantly bearing the news
From which all the many heroes take their cues:

"Sir!"
   "What is it sergeant?"
        "Sir the hordes
March e'en now across the desert swards."

Just like the movies.

Now in the movies
The sergeant's arrival touches off bugles and bells,
Emptying bunks and showers, frightening horses,
Pushing up flags and standards, hardening lines
Of unsoldierly softness, and putting farewells
Hastily in the post so two weeks hence
A perfectly lovely lovely in far-off Canada
Will go pale and bite buttons and stare at the air in Canada.
And in the movies,
Almost before the audience spills its popcorn,
The company's formed and away, with Bim or Kim

Solemnly leading them forth into a sandstorm,
Getting them into what is clearly a trap,
Posting a double guard,
Sending messengers frantic to Marrakech,
Inadvertently pouring the water away,
Losing the ammunition, horses and food
And generally carrying on in the great tradition
By making speeches
Which bring back to mind the glorious name of the Legion,
And serve as the turning point,
After which the Arabs seem doped and perfectly helpless,
Plenty of food is discovered in some old cave,
And reinforcements arrive led by the girl
From Canada.

But in this instance nothing from *Beau Geste*
Or the Paramount lot was attempted,
It being too hot for dramatics,
Even from Kim and Bim,
Aging under the plane trees,
Cursing the food and the bugs, cursing the sergeant
Who gallantly bore the news because he was young,
Full of oats and ignorance, so damned young
In his pretty khaki; nothing at all
(So late in the day, with everyone crocked)
Was attempted despite the sergeant,
Who whirled on his heel, his mission accomplished, and marched,
Hip hip,
Out of the bar, a true trooper, as if to the wars.

So the lights went on and the audience,
Pleasantly stupid, whistled and clapped at the rarity
Of a film breaking down in this late year of Our Lord.

But of course it was not the film; it was not the projector;
Nor was it the man in the booth, who hastened away
As soon as the feature was over, leaving the heroes
Cursing the food and the bugs as heathendom marched,

But some other darker cause having to do
With the script perhaps, or the art,

Or the time,
The time and the place, and how could one blame them,
Seated at iron tables cursing the country.
What could they do,
Seated under the plane trees watching the sergeant
Whirl on his heel, hip hip, in his pretty khaki.
What could they say,
Drinking their gin and bitters by Mount Tessala.
For what after all could be said after all was said
But that the feature had merely run out and the lights had gone on
Because it was time for the lights to go on, and time
For them not to dash out and get lost in the desert
But to rage
As befitted their age
At the drinks and the country, letting their audience
Clap, stamp, whistle and hoot as darkness
Settled on Mount Tessala, the lights went on,
The enemy roamed the desert and everyone itched.

Death

I read of the lords of death in old books:
Of the pyramids and pits
Into which they marched with their wives and best plates,
And lived dead but dressy in heaven nooks;

And of the slaves of death who naked marched to the pits
To serve those lords.
Dully they bowed and duly they lost their heads
And slaved through in the bone as flowerpots.

A democrat myself I read my culture
As the first one to assert man's natural right
To die in his own way at his own rate
So long as he slaves the dying of no other.

Now the real in the mind lives and reads the flesh
And the flesh on the bone lives and reads the bone
And the bone with the marrow lives, reading the marrow —
And none is lord but the lord death live in the marrow,
Holy illiterate, maker, spider of bone.